From Room to Room
The Poetry of Eli Mandel

From Room to Room
The Poetry of Eli Mandel

Selected
with an
introduction by
Peter Webb
and an
afterword by
Andrew Stubbs

lps
LAURIER POETRY SERIES

Wilfrid Laurier University Press

WLU

We acknowledge the support of the Canada Council for the Arts for our publishing program. We acknowledge the financial support of the Government of Canada through the Canada Book Fund for our publishing activities.

Library and Archives Canada Cataloguing in Publication

Mandel, Eli, 1922–1992
  From room to room : the poetry of Eli Mandel / selected, with an introduction by Peter Webb and an afterword by Andrew Stubbs.

(Laurier poetry)
Includes bibliographical references.
Also available in electronic format.
ISBN 978-1-55458-255-6

  I. Webb, Peter, 1968– II. Title. III. Series: Laurier poetry series

PS8526.A52A6 2011   C811'.54   C2010-906489-5

ISBN 978-1-55458-320-1
Electronic format.

  I. Webb, Peter, 1968– II. Title. III. Series: Laurier poetry series (Online)

PS8526.A52A6 2011a   C811'.54   C2010-906490-9

Table of Contents

from *Out of Place*

Foreword

At the beginning of the twenty-first century, poetry in Canada—writing and publishing it, reading and thinking about it—finds itself in a strangely conflicted place. We have many strong poets continuing to produce exciting new work, and there is still a small audience for poetry; but increasingly, poetry is becoming a vulnerable art, for reasons that don't need to be rehearsed.

But there are things to be done: we need more real engagement with our poets. There needs to be more access to their work in more venues—in classrooms, in the public arena, in the media—and there need to be more, and more different kinds, of publications that make the wide range of our contemporary poetry more widely available.

The hope that animates this series from Wilfrid Laurier University Press is that these volumes help to create and sustain the larger readership that contemporary Canadian poetry so richly deserves. Like our fiction writers, our poets are much celebrated abroad; they should just as properly be better known at home.

Our idea is to ask a critic (sometimes herself a poet) to select thirty-five poems from across a poet's career; write an engaging, accessible introduction; and have the poet write an afterword. In this way, we think that the usual practice of teaching a poet through eight or twelve poems from an anthology is much improved upon; and readers in and out of classrooms will have more useful, engaging, and comprehensive introductions to a poet's work. Readers might also come to see more readily, we hope, the connections among, as well as the distances between, the life and the work.

It was the ending of an Al Purdy poem that gave Margaret Laurence the epigraph for *The Diviners*: "but they had their being once / and left a place to stand on." Our poets still do, and they are leaving many places to stand on. We hope that this series helps, variously, to show how and why this is so.

—*Neil Besner*
General Editor

Biographical Note

Elias Wolf ("Eli") Mandel was born in Estevan, Saskatchewan on 3 December 1922 to Charles Isaac Mandel and Eva (Berner) Mandel. His parents were Russian Jewish immigrants who ran a grocery near where Jewish refugees from Russia first established the Hirsch Colony in 1892. In 1935, in the midst of the Great Depression, the Mandels moved to Regina. Eli studied at the city's Collegiate Institute and worked as a pharmacist before serving in the Canadian Medical Corps in Europe from 1943 until the end of World War II.

Following the completion of a B.A. (1949) and an M.A. (1950) at the University of Saskatchewan, Mandel attended the University of Toronto, earning his Ph.D. in 1957 with a dissertation on eighteenth-century English poet Christopher Smart. He taught at Collège Militaire Royal de St. Jean, the University of Alberta, and the University of Calgary before taking a permanent position at Toronto's York University in 1967. In 1949, he married Miriam Minovich, with whom he had two children, Evie and Charles. In 1967, he divorced Miriam and married Ann Hardy, with whom he had a daughter, Sara.

Mandel's first collection, *Trio*, a book shared with Phyllis Webb and Gael Turnbull, appeared in 1954, and his first monograph, *Fuseli Poems*, came out in 1960. *Black and Secret Man* followed in 1964. An *Idiot Joy* (1967), winner of the Governor General's Award for poetry (a prize shared with Alden Nowlan's *Bread, Wine and Salt*), bolstered Mandel's national reputation, as did two books published in 1973, *Stony Plain* and *Crusoe: Poems Selected and New* (edited by Margaret Atwood and Dennis Lee). Mandel's poetic maturity peaked in 1977 with *Out of Place*, a poem sequence featuring a preface and photographs by Ann, inspired by a visit to the remains of the Hirsch and Hoffer Jewish colonies outside Estevan. A final monograph, *Life Sentence: Poems and Journals, 1976–1980* (1981), reflects Mandel's extensive travels around Asia, Europe, and South America. Numerous other poems remained unpublished until 2000, when they appeared with earlier work in the two-volume *The Other Harmony: The Collected Poetry of Eli Mandel* (edited by Andrew Stubbs and Judy Chapman).

Mandel was also a prolific anthologist and literary critic. Anthologies he edited or co-edited include *Poetry 62* (with Jean-Guy Pilon), *Contexts of Canadian Criticism* (1971), and *Poets of Contemporary Canada, 1960–1970* (1972). His critical works include *Irving Layton* (1969) and the essay collections *Criticism: The Silent-Speaking Words* (1966), *Another Time* (1977), and *The*

Family Romance (1986). Mandel's criticism addresses a wide range of subjects, including modern poetry and fiction, Victorian poetry, Jewish culture, the Holocaust, post-impressionist art, and the mythic legacy of the Canadian west.

Mandel's fellow writers and critics paid tribute to his life and work in a double issue of *Essays on Canadian Writing* (Winter 1991/Spring 1992) and in *The Politics of Art: Eli Mandel's Poetry and Criticism* (edited by Ed Jewinski and Andrew Stubbs, 1992). After more than four decades of creative activity, Mandel's remarkable life ended on 3 September 1992.

Introduction

The past decade has seen a resurgence of interest in major Canadian poets of the twentieth century, with new volumes and critical studies of Leonard Cohen, Louis Dudek, Irving Layton, A.M. Klein, Dorothy Livesay, and Al Purdy appearing regularly. For Eli Mandel, a prolific contemporary of these other luminaries, recovery has been more elusive. He was, to borrow Richard Kostelanetz's description of Mandel's American contemporary John Ashbery, "a difficult poet"—destined more for critical acclaim than popular acceptance.

"[H]ow could you contain me?" Mandel's speaker asks twice in "The Meaning of the I CHING," the first poem in the Governor General's Award–winning collection *An Idiot Joy* (1967). The only possible answer: one *cannot* contain him. Generic categories like "modernist," "postmodernist," "regionalist," "prairie poet," and "Jewish poet" may suit particular poems by Mandel, but none describes his work as a whole. He belonged to no school or movement, though he drew influence from many. For Robert Kroetsch, he was "the poet as Houdini, finding his way out of chains, and then back in again" (10). How much this mercurial quality has affected his legacy is hard to say—critics, teachers, anthologists, and publishers of poetry all use literary categories to shape their activities. Whatever the case, Mandel's resistance to labels is crucial in appreciating the formal complexity and thematic richness of his work.

Mandel's arsenal of imagery and allusion is unusually diverse. "Estevan Saskatchewan," an early poem from the collection *Trio* (1954), combines references to Cain, Oedipus, and the characters of *Hamlet* in a poem about Mandel's birthplace during the Great Depression. "In the Caves of My City," from *Fuseli Poems* (1960), hinges on the Hebrew Bible and William Blake and then, in the final stanza, on Charlie Chaplin and the silent cinema. "The Fire Place" and "Epilogue," from the same collection, contain gothic and psychological imagery reminiscent of Edgar Allan Poe, Sigmund Freud, and the eighteenth-century painter Henry Fuseli. "Minotaur Poems" is equally gothic, set in a dreamscape populated by mythical beings drawn from Ovid's *Metamorphosis* and other classical sources. Recent history is equally alive in Mandel's work. In "Doll on a Mantelpiece," the bombings of Dresden and Berlin during World War II disrupt a poetic still life where "[a]ll is still, chill, white." "On the 25th Anniversary of the Liberation of Auschwitz" and "On the Renewal of Bombing in VietNam December, 1972," both from *Stony Plain*

(1973), are searing evocations of war and genocide that acknowledge the inadequacies of poetic language in representing the horrors of the modern age. Mandel's later work, in *Out of Place* (1977) and *Life Sentence* (1981), continues to test the reader's ability to unravel allusions, uncover meaning, and trace the relationships among poetry, experience, and memory.

Mandel's poetry has been known to challenge even the most sophisticated readers. Northrop Frye, on first encountering *Trio*, found Mandel's poetry "much more difficult to follow" than that of his co-contributors to the book, Gael Turnbull and Phyllis Webb (255). Dennis Cooley, a long-time admirer and perceptive critic of Mandel's work, remarks that in the early books "the poems required special efforts on the part of readers in order to interpret them" because "few people were equipped to read them, and those who could were able to extract meaning only through enormous effort." Critic Ann Munton, finding Mandel's early poems "literary, convoluted, and often obscure," describes later work in *Life Sentence* as writing which "pushes poetry to its border" and "is not a poetry for the fainthearted" (1). Lastly, Margaret Atwood, who co-edited *Crusoe: Poems Selected and New* (1973) with Dennis Lee, likens Mandel's work to "a trip to inner space, the consciousness cut adrift in its own void" (58).

"Poets," Mandel wrote in *Poets of Contemporary Canada, 1960–1970*, "do not produce poetry for the convenience of editors of anthologies. So long as they continue to write, they defy our critical wisdom, confound our attempts at precise description, and redefine not only the past of our literature but their own past as well" (Introduction x). Mandel refers here to the work of such contemporaries as Cohen, Layton, and Purdy, yet the tendency to "confound our attempts at precise description" applies even better to his own work. Unlike Cohen, Mandel wrote no populist overtures to the sixties (the one exception, *Stony Plain's* "For Jimmy Hendrix and Janis Joplin," misspells Jimi's first name). His public persona was not outrageous like Layton's and his poems lacked the effortless ribaldry of Purdy's humorous works. Yet as Mandel writes in "The Meaning of the I CHING," he too was "crazed by poetry"—consumed by a desire to articulate the world through verse.

Rarely do form and genre in Mandel's work remain stable for the sake of editorial "convenience." "Minotaur Poems" for example works as both a single poem in six parts and a sequence of six distinct poems. Manuscripts held at the University of Manitoba archives show that "Minotaur Poems" began as a three-stanza work entitled "Poetry of Action," and in later stages of composition incorporated both "The Minotaur" (an early work from Mandel's student days) and "Estevan Saskatchewan." By the time it appeared in *Trio*, "Minotaur

Poems" was a six-part poem, although the title is oddly positioned at the head of Mandel's section of the book as if referring to his entire contribution to the volume. Moreover, the sixth part of "Minotaur Poems" is headed by both a Roman numeral, "VI," and a subtitle, "Orpheus," furthering the ambiguity. In A.J.M. Smith's landmark anthology, *The Oxford Book of Canadian Verse* (1960), Parts I, II, and VI are presented as stand-alone poems, while Mandel's own *Dreaming Backwards* (1981) uses "Minotaur Poems" as a *chapter title* for a sequence that again includes "Estevan Saskatchewan." Finally, the posthumous collection *The Other Harmony: The Collected Poetry of Eli Mandel* (2000) enforces the unity of the six-part sequence, allowing "Estevan Saskatchewan" to stand alone. Frank Davey draws further attention to the "triple existence" of "Minotaur Poems" by querying the ambiguity of the title: "does it announce poems by the minotaur, for the minotaur, about the minotaur, or resembling in some way the minotaur?"

Such formal puzzles are unlikely to bother readers encountering "Minotaur Poems" in one particular version (such as the six-part sequence presented in this book). But they highlight the multiplicity of possible readings inherent in Mandel's work. Practically every one of his poems presents complexities and ambiguities—a tangled phrase here, a sudden gap there, a reference or allusion demanding one reach for Homer, the Bible, a volume of Shakespeare or Blake. Photographs, paintings, symphonies, newsreels, silent films, and popular westerns—all these, too, are part of Mandel's insistence on the links between poetry and wider cultural experience.

"Modern poetry is international in style and radical in its attitudes," Mandel claims in the 1977 essay collection *Another Time* (86). Once again, a statement meant to describe others—a manifesto against a poetics limited by local colour and parochial themes—is epitomized by Mandel himself. Mandel wrote much poetry centred on the local, but all of it radically transcends the conventions of regionalism. In *Out of Place*, Mandel's book-length poetry cycle about his rural-Saskatchewan heritage, "doors of perception" (drawing on yet another allusion, to Aldous Huxley) take both the poet and reader beyond the nostalgia for things past. Variations in form—found poems, broken syntax, meditations on photographs, tombstones, and petroglyphs—disrupt linearity and inhibit closure. In "signs," the speaker transcends an "indescribable border" between place and memory:

> whatever has been hidden here
> remains of speech
>   the town lives
> in its syntax we are ghosts.

Having grown up in an age of war, violence, and socio-economic uncertainty, Mandel had many "ghosts" to contend with. The Jewish community around Estevan had been established by survivors of pogroms that tore through Russia in the wake of Alexander II's 1881 assassination, which was falsely blamed on Jewish conspirators. Mandel's parents, who fled the Ukraine before his birth, did their best to raise him "as a genteel Victorian boy, with a quaint though serious touch of middle-European Yiddish gentility to boot." But the Depression-ravaged environment of rural Saskatchewan also made him "a sensuous little savage" who "tortured gophers" and "pored over the corset ads in the Eaton's catalogue, all in the sweaty, thick closeness of the childhood dream" (*Another Time 73*). In 1935, around the time the Mandels moved to Regina, reports of a new and deadlier scourge against Jews began flowing from Nazi Germany. Eight years later, while serving in the Canadian Medical Corps in Europe, Mandel witnessed the violence of the Second World War at first hand.

Although his postwar life was peaceful by comparison, Mandel's early experiences influenced the stark depictions of violence and persecution inhabiting many of his poems. "Minotaur Poems," for all its dream-like and mythic imagery, has lines that evoke warlike scenes of carnage and trauma:

> I have gone from room to room
> asking the janitors who were sweeping up
> the brains that lay on the floors,
> the bones shining in the wastebaskets,
> and once I asked a suit of clothes
> that collapsed at my breath and bundled
> and crawled on the floor like a coward.

Broken and mutilated bodies, psychological confusion, figures emptied of strength and moral assurance—these are hallmarks of a poet deeply influenced by the "age of extremes," as the historian Eric Hobsbawm termed the period corresponding with Mandel's life.

"Any account of the unrealizable is, in some sense, a failure, a trivialization. How is it possible to convey what is impossible to convey?" (Mandel, "Auschwitz" 216). The Holocaust, the bombing of Dresden, the Vietnam War, the JFK assassination, the Chilean coup of 1973, Argentina's Dirty War—all these events happened during Mandel's adult life, yet he was a direct witness to none of them. For a poet of social conscience and historical awareness, problems of representation become acute when the urge to express clashes with the limitations of knowledge. The ancient Greeks called this phenomenon *adynaton*—"the impossibility of addressing oneself adequately to the topic" (Vickers qtd. in McLoughlin 15). Yet as untrustworthy as language can be, to avoid representation altogether—to write "no poetry after Auschwitz," as George Steiner (inaccurately) paraphrased Theodor Adorno (53)—is for Mandel not an option. "A reticent language, one that will not say certain words because they have been spoiled or are wicked or debased, simply confirms the possibility of bestiality" (*Another Time* 39). For Mandel the way out was to write self-reflexive poems that defy literary convention, beginning "a process of personal and formal dissolution, the breaking apart of personal, psychological *structures*, and moral categories, the imperative of tradition" ("Auschwitz" 216). *Derealization*, Mandel called this process. But the term is less important than its effects on his poetry. Broken lines and jagged columns; gaps between, and within, words; shifting voices, perspectives, and time frames—these are emblems of a writer anxious to document his own struggles with representation.

Mandel's postwar years of study at the University of Saskatchewan and the University of Toronto were as important to his poetry as his tumultuous youth, steeping him in the world traditions of literature and philosophy, which provided an endless fount of material from which to draw. His fascination with myth, allusion, and the metaphysical, forged by his reading of Homer, Plato, Confucianism, the Bible, Shakespeare, Blake, and Christopher Smart (the eighteenth-century poet whose feminine alter ego inspired Mandel's "Mary Midnight's Prologue" and a later verse drama), bred a literary style different from that of other prairie authors of the postwar period. One of his admired teachers at the University of Saskatchewan, the novelist Edward McCourt, established a critical foundation for prairie literature in his landmark study *The Canadian West in Fiction* (1949). For McCourt, a classic realist raised on Joseph Conrad and Thomas Hardy, the writer must be "a pictorial artist able to describe accurately the physical features of a characteristic prairie landscape" (55). This aesthetic suited McCourt's own fiction, as it did that of forebears such as Frederick Philip Grove, W.O. Mitchell, and Sinclair Ross. But Mandel was a poet, not a novelist, so "pictorial" realism was not an option if he was to write anything beyond documentaries in verse. Although his upbringing in some ways resembled those of Brian O'Connal in Mitchell's *Who Has Seen the Wind* (1947) and Michael Troy in McCourt's *Walk Through the Valley* (1958), Mandel's Jewish heritage, years at war, and relocation to Toronto made it impossible to situate himself in a strictly local, regionalist aesthetic. Moreover, "realism or accuracy," Mandel maintained, "fails, because accuracy of fact and tone is essentially superficial" (*Another Time* 48). His critical appreciation of Freud, Frye, and Leslie Fiedler—all theorists of myth and the imaginary—made mythic representations of the world as authentic to him as McCourt's "pictorial" landscape. "Creating its own space and time," Mandel wrote, "a mythic geography reveals the mask of imagination, a primitive blood-streaked face" (*Another Time* 85).

Such dramatic pronouncements typify Mandel's views of his own work. But neither he nor his critics sufficiently acknowledged a lyrical quality in his poetry that transcends its more technically challenging aspects. Throughout Mandel's work one encounters poems that arrest the emotions and take account of brief and striking moments in time. "City Park Merry-Go-Round," for example, uses the traditional form of the villanelle (a romantic French form best represented in English by Dylan Thomas's "Do Not Go Gentle into That Good Night") to evoke the conflict between the innocence of childhood and the existential doubts of adulthood. The skilful match between subject (the merry-go-round with its circular motion) and form (the patterned rhymes and repeating lines of the villanelle) highlight Mandel's ability to work within highly disciplined structures.

Elegy is another form in which he excelled. "Charles Isaac Mandel," an elegy for his orthodox father, is comparable to A.M. Klein's "Heirloom" as a meditation on a son's coming to terms with a father's modest legacy. "Two Dream Songs for John Berryman" is a troubled lament for the American poet who killed himself by jumping from the Washington Avenue Bridge in Minneapolis in 1972. And "In My 57th Year" is a stark and anxious poem about the death of two parents and the bittersweet process of watching children grow and leave home. Readers who explore Mandel's work beyond this brief volume will find other excellent examples of the elegiac and confessional in his large corpus.

Mandel's work continued to change and develop until the end of his life. Among numerous poems left unpublished upon his death in 1992, one of the most interesting is "Zenith: Saving to Disk." Mandel took an interest in the home-computer revolution of the 1980s, purchasing an Indian-made Zenith PC and participating in *SwiftCurrent*, the seminal online literary journal edited by Frank Davey and Fred Wah. Concerned with the nebulous nature of language in the digital age, "Zenith: Saving to Disk" imagines the poet as a "ghost" subsumed by a hyperreal world of bits and bytes:

figures on a screen
illusions dreams
of words dreamt by me:

the absence of my self
the absent self who writes
the ghostly writing self

Dreaming, alternate realities, and the dissolution of self: these themes recall "Minotaur Poems," written four decades earlier, highlighting a thematic continuity that transcends formal difference. Illusion replacing reality, new media dominating culture, and the dissipation of the individual conscience are ideas commonplace in the wake of Jean Baudrillard, Neil Postman, and other theorists of the post-Internet era. Mandel died before this discourse and most of its terminology came of age, but his concern with such matters ahead of the curve shows his characteristic willingness to divine new thematic realms with an eye to the future. As his poetry could not be "contained," neither could his imagination.

—*Peter Webb*

Works Cited

Atwood, Margaret. *Second Words: Selected Critical Prose, 1960–1982*. Toronto: Anansi, 1982. Print.

Cooley, Dennis. "The First Four Books." *Essays on Canadian Writing* 45/46 (1991–1992): n. pag. *Academic Search Premier*. Web. 7 June 2010.

Davey, Frank. "'Minotaur Poems': Language, Form, and Centre in Eli Mandel's Poetry." *Essays on Canadian Writing* 45/46 (1991–1992): n. pag. *Academic Search Premier*. Web. 7 June 2010.

Frye, Northrop. "Letters in Canada: 1954." *University of Toronto Quarterly* 24.3 (1955): 254–55. Print.

Hobsbawm, Eric. *The Age of Extremes: The Short Twentieth Century, 1914–1991*. London: Abacus, 1994. Print.

Kostelanetz, Richard. "How to Be a Difficult Poet." *New York Times Magazine* 23 May 1976: n. pag. *ProQuest Historical Newspapers: The New York Times (1851–2006)*. Web. 7 June 2010.

Kroetsch, Robert. Preface. *Dreaming Backwards: The Selected Poetry of Eli Mandel*. By Eli Mandel. Don Mills, ON: General Publishing, 1981. 9–12. Print.

Mandel, Eli. *Another Time*. Erin, ON: Porcépic, 1977. Print.

———. "Auschwitz: Poetry of Alienation." *Canadian Literature* 100 (1984): 213–18. Print.

———. Introduction. *Poets of Contemporary Canada, 1960–1970*. Ed. Mandel. Toronto: McClelland and Stewart, 1972. x–xvi. Print.

McCourt, Edward. *The Canadian West in Fiction*. Toronto: Ryerson, 1949. Print.

McLoughlin, Kate. "War and Words." *The Cambridge Companion to War Writing*. Ed. McLoughlin. Cambridge: Cambridge UP, 2009. 15–24. Print.

Munton, Ann. "The Aesthetics of Silence in Mandel's Recent Poetry." *The Politics of Art: Eli Mandel's Poetry and Criticism*. Ed. Ed Jewinski and Andrew Stubbs. Amsterdam: Rodopi, 1992. 1–9. Print.

Steiner, George. *Language and Silence: Essays on Language, Literature, and the Inhuman*. New York: Atheneum, 1967. Print.

Minotaur Poems

I

It has been hours in these rooms,
the opening to which, door or sash,
I have lost. I have gone from room to room
asking the janitors who were sweeping up
the brains that lay on the floors,
the bones shining in the wastebaskets,
and once I asked a suit of clothes
that collapsed at my breath and bundled
and crawled on the floor like a coward.
Finally, after several stories,
in the staired and eyed hall,
I came upon a man with the face of a bull.

II

My father was always out in the garage
building a shining wing, a wing
that curved and flew along the edge of blue air
in that streamed and sunlit room
that smelled of oil and engines
and crankcase grease, and especially
the lemon smell of polish and cedar.
Outside there were sharp rocks, and trees,
cold air where birds fell like rocks
and screams, hawks, kites, and cranes.
The air was filled with a buzzing and flying
and the invisible hum of a bee's wings was honey
in my father's framed and engined mind.
Last Saturday we saw him at the horizon
screaming like a hawk as he fell into the sun.

III

They chose among us in the fall of the year,
by lot, behind fierce masks designed of sign
to ward off the imminent descent of the sun people;
someone talked of a dying god, as if
the young ones among us believed in that
any more, others cautioned us against the voices
we were always supposed to hear and these
were stubborn about the women crying.
I remembered the face of the one who brought me here
when they drew my name in the hall,
it was her persuasions in the beginning,
something about fathers.
                                    Like the others, before this
I saw only their breasts that appeared on the walls,
legs moving in unison, the swaying of sweat-stained
bodies and their half closed eyes:
all the talk about signs when I knew
the boys were only waiting for the time
when the women undressed, as they always did,
                                    snickering
in those same fields that make a dawn in vision
where birds begin to live in rocks and screams.
It is hard to feel free of accusation
because of eyes
although there is a difference between revelation
and action bellied into life, between
believing in voices
and knowing the chances that we have to take.

IV

Now I am dressed in a multitude of rooms
like a Chinese box, and slip from covers

into covers   Dawn will not help me nor
the day's exposure   I am a prodigious pun
to hide and show myself between these walls
this otherwise where sunlight
dressed in a tweed suit pursues me
or a stranger in the rooms
                and footfalls on the stairs
and eyes   and over all
      the whispering and chattering of the walls
            the pipes and hammered arteries of the place.

Is that a revelation in a field of light
competing with a shadow on the rock?
A bird's shadow seen from here?
Or a cloud between the sky and land
footed and patterned into phrases?

It is hours since I have been in here.
If I had once seen anything
except birds,
rocks, land, and all winter long
                        the ice and snow

                        V

Within these walls I am to look for light
Or hold an abstract in my hand as firm
As apples or the golden bar the older men
Returned to us. Remember that. That spring
There were those crowds and crowds below the cliffs
This side of town and all along the beach,
Flags out, booths filled with toys, and one,
The better salesman of the lot, a beggar
From the north had miniatures of bars
That went like hotcakes. Fleece for the crowd.

A replica to keep you as it kept our men
This winter past. Then noise, flocks wheeling overhead,
The painted ship, a bauble on the sea, came like a toy
To harbour.

          And the tall bronzed men descended
Between the cheers and speeches at the harbour mouth,
Talk about campaigns in lands we'd never heard of,
Cheers and lewd remarks and laughter, the look
In other eyes, and counting of the crew
And stooping at the gaps aghast.
That was another death, the shock in surf,
The rock's point of view, the hawk
Momentarily composing before the fall
His target of a landscape from the sky.
The trailing plume before the dark.
Night on the beach and smoke
                from the new charred campfires.

VI

Orpheus

The Welshman by the pit whose Sabbath voice
Would set the week to peace, or end a day,
Picked over coal and said he knew within
The inside of our god, his transformation
Out of tree, the face in black, faced out of coal,
Stamped on the walls he picked. His useful metaphor,
He said, the pit shaped underneath him into black
And pitied words that moved the leaves or sang
Together flocks, or shook the dull and herded animals.
His pity also took between the rocks

Some still alive who saw the black and second
Hand that clawed them, and he mocked in Welsh
Whatever shades fell back, and cursed and sang
Back to their second death   those grave ghosts.

Who found his body and who found his head
And who wiped god from off his eyes and face?

Estevan Saskatchewan

A small town bears the mark of Cain,
Or the oldest brother with the dead king's wife
In a foul relation as viewed by sons,
Lies on the land, squat, producing
Love's queer offspring only,
Which issue drives the young
To feign a summer madness, consort with skulls,
While the farmer's chorus, a Greek harbinger,
Forecasts by frost or rings about the moon
How ill and black the seeds will grow.

This goodly frame, the earth, each of its sons,
With nature as a text, and common theme
The death of fathers, anguished in betrayal
From the first family returns a sacrifice
Of blood's brother, a splintered eyeball
Groined in the fields, scarecrow to crows.
This warns Ophelia to her morning song,
Bawdy as a lyric in a pretty brain gone bad,
While on those fields the stupid harvest lies.

The Fire Place

A furnace is of stone and clay,
A fire burns inside the stone,
Beside the flame Fuseli lay,
The heart within it was his own.

Fuseli, when the witch came in,
Raised the roof above his stone,
On her thighs he painted sin,
On her head a horse's mane.

From her lips a vocal moth
Issued screaming to the smoke,
Augustan ladies in their mirth
Gathered folds about her smock.

In the smoking cup a sea,
By the bed a painted ship,
In the door a massive key,
On the floor an open trap.

Coupled with a horse a man
Leans upon her breast and sighs,
Flaming curtains issue then,
Thus between the witch's thighs.

In the Caves of My City

If I said that in the caves of our city
I have seen these eyes glare, and the bent gaze
like a pin, or a sun orbiting a dark and silent moon,
and the clenched brow, a fist like Job's or Blake's
to hammer iron language into shape

                              or that the mouth
roared like the rustle of paper, or the sigh of elms
sick with the dutch disease, or the sound made by dikes
at the thought of the sea piling its green lava
onto the hissing towns,

                    would you then shrug
and say: animals have visions, the beast
is not at ease until he's clean.

                    Dirt?
You look at your nails: the horns of Jericho,
Joshua once clawed down walls, Isaiah shrieked
a mouthful of dikes at Leviathan (hooked him
on a simile shaped like a beak, hung him
on its barb).

                    The word. I see her summer dress
lift, in the white of her skin, a leprous snow,
the red slash of the sun smiles below
her bruised blue brow.

                    Must I become Chaplin
to praise and save her? My tongue flickers
like a newsreel, and with epileptic grace
I lurch through the twenties of my mind,
a celluloid hero, fabulous as a Basilisk
who pins me in the caves of my city.

City Park Merry-Go-Round

Freedom is seldom what you now believe.
Mostly you circle round and round the park:
Night follows day, these horses never leave.

Like children, love whatever you conceive,
See then your world as lights whirled in the dark.
Freedom is seldom what you now believe.

Your world moves up and down or seems to weave
And still you pass and pass that same old mark.
Night follows day, these horses never leave.

You thought your past was here, you might retrieve
That wild illusion whirling in the dark.
Freedom is seldom what you now believe.

Sick on that circle you begin to grieve.
You wish the ride would end and you could park.
Night follows day, these horses never leave.

Mostly you circle round and round the park.
You'd give your life now to be free to leave.
Freedom is seldom what you now believe.
Night follows day, these horses never leave.

Doll on the Mantelpiece

Here on the mantel where a Dresden doll
Looks into a frozen german hill
All is still, chill, white,
Except the red stain on her lips,
The blood of colour there.

She is poised for a dance above the fire,
A hand out for a partner neither here
Nor anywhere. The fire breathes below
A savage noise of wood and she looks out
Over the white hill, still as a doll,
Chill in her world of ivory.

Why do I think of clowns, of emperors,
Of Nietzsche in his tower and all Berlin
Falling in flames while this silly doll
Stands on a fire, calm beside a frozen hill?

Epilogue

When our mayor was put out to eat grass
And on the street manholes opened like eyes,
Everyone said it had come from below
Because the street was nervous, empty,
And the sewers rumbled for days, the wires
Sang in the high wind and cracks appeared
In the gray cement like folds in an elephant's hide.

Everyone said it had come from below
Because the banks toppled over like great gods
And fire flamed out of the mouth of the stock exchange,
And our bird-like mayor, like a hoofed thing,
Galloped away to the green fields in the country.

Mary Midnight's Prologue

I don't doubt that I prefer London, 1763,
Though why I was born there baffles me.
I seem to remember hop-fields in Kent
Before the darkness fell on me in Lent.

But someone called me in my cave
And now emerged in light, my love,
I come to embrace you in my pantaloons
And my almanac wisdom in my belly's balloon.

Inside me you will find all wisdom,
The magazine before catalogue and doom
Where I unpage the universal heart
Of continental tears and provinces of hurt.

Do not be afraid of my vulvular mouth.
Such darkness was before the dust.
Such darkness will be after wrath.
In such darkness will be after birth.

I have swallowed other poets in other times.
My uterus is seminal with rhymes.
You think your present is your singing past.
I know the darkness is the future lost.

Now I shall become your landscape
Now the towns of your eyes will collapse
Now you will join your body's slough
To the water of mother of all the dead.

Charles Isaac Mandel

Those uplands of the suburban mind,
sunlit, where dwell the lithe ironists,
athletic as greeks, boy-lovers,
mathematical in love as in science.
Formalists. What have I to do with them?
I gather the few relics of my father:
his soiled Tallis, his Tefillin,
the strict black leather of his dark faith.

David

all day the gopher-killing boys
    their sling-shot arms
        their gopher-cries

the king insisting
    my poetry must stop

I have written nothing since May

instead
      walk among the boys
gopher-blood on their stretched
hands
      murder will end murder
the saying goes, someone must
do something about the rodents
and poems do not:
             even the doctors
admit that it's plague
ask me about my arms
        look
at my shadow hanging
  like a slingshot

the world turns like a murderous stone
    my forehead aching with stars

Hippolytus

In the unknowable space between this room
and the running mane of the horizon
where dimmer than thunder the clouds
shudder and toss under the wind's whip
I have been dreaming of horses

I have known mothers larger than boxcars
carrying the freight of years and wars
toward some stockyard of their minds
where they can count the slaughtered time

I too know something of punishment
there have been drownings even here
beside the dry reeds of the lakeless fields
hands have been held out to me
I dare not touch beside that unseen water
and once a beaten animal stumbled by
looking like someone's brother

easier then to praise passion
the strong in one another's arms
testing the machinery of love
the freight that moves the world's
horizons
          everyone knows the rules
what to ignore, when and how to whip
the beaten and to bruise the animals

at the edge of these dark waters
hearing the drums of the world movers
again begins the sound of hoofs
and I see the wet heaving horses of a last rain

The Meaning of the I CHING

unopened
　　　　book of old men
　　　　orange-blossom book
　　　　　　　　　　　before me
you were
　　　　how could you contain me?

do you not see I am the mouths
of telegraphs and cemeteries?
my mother groaned like the whole
of Western Union to deliver
my message
　　　　　　and yelling birthdays
that unrolled from my lungs
like ticker-tape for presidents
about to be murdered
　　　　　　　　I sped
on a line that flew
to the vanishing point of the west

before I was
　　　　　you were
unopened book
　　　　　do not craze me
with the odour of orange-blossom

do not sit there
like smiling old men

　　　　how could you contain me?

under my fingers words form themselves
it's crazy to talk of temples in this day
but light brightens on my page
like today moving against the wooden house
all shapes change and yet stay
as if they were marble in autumn
as if in the marbled yellow autumn
each western house becomes a shrine
stiff against the age of days
under my fingers stiffly formed

one cannot be another, I cry,
let me not be crazed by poetry

I will walk in streets that vanish
noting peculiar elms like old women
who will crash under the storm of sun
that breaks elm, woman, man
into a crumble of stump and bark
until the air is once more clear
in the sane emptiness of fall

iii

my body speaks to me
as my arms say: two are one
as my feet say: earth upon earth
as my knees say: bow down, unhinge yourself
as my cells say: we repeat the unrepeatable

the book speaks: arrange yourself in the form
                     that will arrange you

before I was: colours that hurt me
                         arranged themselves in me

before I was: horizons that blind me
                         arranged themselves in me

before I was: the dead who speak to me
                         arranged themselves in me

iv

I am the mouths
of smiling old men

there rises from me
the scent of orange-blossoms

I speak in the words
of the ancient dead

arranged
in the raging sun
in the stiffening age of days

and in the temple of my house

one becomes another
I am crazed by poetry

Girl on a High Wire

Do you think I'd sit here staring
if I knew how to invent chair-lifts
or lacked this odd taste for vertigo?

What if I dare you to jump, saying, ah
my hurt bird, I will catch you—
and if I weren't there (someone calling,
my son pointing at camels or wanting
to pee) when your eyes became horizons?
Or if you fell
into the well of bankers, mid-wives,
my brother-in-law, the Prudential Life
Insurance Company?
                              I see them,
heroine, hefting you, their applause
ringing your head with the clatter of zircons,
mouths blowing little balloons of praise.

The great globe circles.
Soldiers fall into muddy rivers.
Boys walk the tightrope of their prison yard.

I can no longer look at telephone wires,
the vanishing point of your unfinished portrait.

I shall devote myself to entomology,
practise weight-lifting with dinky toys,
but who will keep me from my crooked prayers,
those mad doves that fling haloes around you?

Houdini

I suspect he knew that trunks are metaphors,
could distinguish between the finest rhythms
unrolled on rope or singing in a chain
and knew the metrics of the deepest pools

I think of him listening to the words
spoken by manacles, cells, handcuffs,
chests, hampers, roll-top desks, vaults,
especially the deep words spoken by coffins

escape, escape: quaint Harry in his suit
his chains, his desk, attached to all attachments
how he'd sweat in that precise struggle
with those binding words, wrapped around him
like that mannered style, his formal suit

and spoken when? by whom? What thing first said
"there's no way out?"; so that he'd free himself,
leap, squirm, no matter how, to chain himself again,
once more jump out of the deep alive
with all his chains singing around his feet
like the bound crowds who sigh, who sigh.

The Madness of Our Polity

Being savages, we learn to bow and smile
And choke behind our showing teeth
Those howls that echo from the fields of sleep.

I saw this. On the prairies where I lived
a boy who put a needle in a gopher's eye
knew more of civil law than all my friends.

What other emblems do you need?

The Speaking Earth

grandfathers fall into it
their mighty beards muffled in grass

and admirals, the sea-sounding men

lovers fall into the earth
like rain on wet dark bodies

listen, our lady earth flowers
into the sea-green language
of grass and drowned admirals

listen: in bearded branches
clasped like broken hands
admiring birds
lovers singing of their kiss
before and after all the words

From the North Saskatchewan

when on the high bluff discovering
the river cuts below
                  send messages
we have spoken to those on the boats

I am obsessed by the berries they eat
all night odour of Saskatoon
and an unidentifiable odour
something baking
               the sun
never reaches the lower bank

I cannot read the tree markings

today the sky is torn by wind:
a field after a long battle
strewn with corpses of cloud

give blessings to my children
speak for us to those who sent us here
say we did all that could be done
we have not learned
what lies north of the river
or past those hills that look like beasts

Two Dream Songs for John Berryman

1

Henry, it says to me here
you took yourself to a bridge.
And you, weary and wavery,
walked, bone and brain, all
to the rail
            there perched
waved farewell from rail

Is that how it was done?

Is it only possible to live
how we have done backwards
dreaming our way from death to
bony life?
            Well, it was gaily
done
        but, here on the coast of Spain,
heartsick like you
                        and hurt too
by burning poems that will not write
themselves I
            say
now fare-you-well
with Sylvia, Ted, Randall,
and all your hurt friends,

God notwithstanding

2

It is done but not done well
Henry   to betake yourself to ice
and death in a Minnesota morning

or a bruise
throwing yourself from bridge
to ice
        why would you want so
to say to me or to God once more
that nothing is fair
among fair women and hardy men

to God
        who never once cared
now name him as you will

it's both night and day
not done well to you or anyone
less or better
                not well

On the 25th Anniversary of the Liberation of Auschwitz: Memorial Services, Toronto, January 25, 1970 YMHA Bloor & Spadina

the name is hard
a German sound made out of
the gut guttural throat
y scream yell ing open
voice mouth growl
                    and sweat
"the only way out of Auschwitz
is through the chimneys"
                        of course
that's second hand   that's told
again   Sigmund Sherwood (Sobolewski)
twisting himself into that sentence
before us on the platform
                        the poem
shaping itself late in the after
noon later than it would be:

Pendericki's "Wrath of God"
moaning electronic Polish theatric
the screen silent
                    framed by the name
looking away from/pretending not there
no   name   no   not   name no

        Auschwitz
    in GOTHIC lettering
                    the hall
a parody a reminiscence a nasty memory
the Orpheum in Estevan before Buck Jones
the Capitol in Regina before Tom Mix

waiting for the guns
waiting for the cowboy killers
one two three
            Legionnaires
Polish ex-prisoners Association
Legions
          their medals their flags
so the procession, the poem gradual
ly insistent beginning to shape itself
with the others
            walked with them
into the YMHA Bloor & Spadina
thinking apocalypse shame degradation
thinking bones and bodies melting
thickening thinning melting bones and bodies
thinking not mine / must speak clearly
the poet's words / Yevtyshenko at Baba-Yar

there   this January   snow
heavy wet   the wind   heavy wet
the street grey white slush melted concrete
bones and bodies melting slush
                 saw
with the others
          the prisoner
in the YMHA hall Bloor & Spadina
arms wax stiff body stiff unnatural
coloured face blank eyes
            walked
with the others toward the screen
toward the picture
          SLIDES
     this is mother
     this is father
     this is
          the one who is
waving her arms like that

is the one who
           like
I mean running with her breasts bound
ing
      running
                 with her hands here and there
with her here and
                    there
hands
        that   that is
the poem becoming the body
becoming the faint hunger
ing body
          prowling
                    through
words the words words the words
opening   mouths ovens
the generals smiling saluting
in their mythic uniforms god-like
generals uniforms with the black leather
with the straps and the intricate leather
the phylacteries and the prayer shawl
corsets and the boots and the leather straps

and the shining faces of the generals in their boots
and their stiff wax bodies their unnatural faces
and their blank eyes and their hands their stiff hands
and the generals in their straps and wax and stiff
staying standing
                  melting bodies and thickening
                  quick flesh on flesh handling
                  hands

the poem flickers, fades
the four Yarzeit candles guttering one
        each four million lights dim
my words drift
                smoke from chimneys and ovens
        a bad picture, the power failing
    pianist clattering on and over and through
the long Saturday afternoon in the Orpheum
        while the whitehatted star spangled cowboys
            shot the dark men and shot the dark men
            and we threw popcorn balls and grabbed
            each other and cheered:
                        me jewboy yelling
for the shot town and the falling men
        and the lights come on
                        and

        with the others
standing in silence

the gothic word hangs
over us on a shroud-white screen

and we drift away
                to ourselves
                    to the late Sunday Times
                    the wet snow
                    the city

                    a body melting

Room XV

If you walk into Room XV of the Prado in Madrid you will see there the most marvellous painting in the world. The painter, Velasquez, stands at his easel, a delightful blonde princess, accompanied by her maids in waiting, stands to his left and in front of him, to her left a dwarf lady and a dog, behind them other attendants, and at the back of the room, past a mirror that reflects two who are looking toward the painter, an official opens a door to allow more light to enter. Look closely and you will see that the spectators in the room XV are so life-like that at first you do not notice the layers of pigment making up their faces, the extraordinary application of paint to limb and cloth, the cunningly calculated placing and perspectives, the miraculous creation of even the atmosphere. So splendid is the illusion that you could easily believe these figures walk, talk amongst themselves, and go from room to room in the great museum to be admired by other paintings, as the Maids of Honour admire us.

On the Renewal of Bombing
in VietNam December, 1972

At the sight of this photograph
forming itself out of headlines and print
what should a poet do but cry out
that the dead are no less real
for falling into pictures of ruined cities

I do not mean to speak as a prophet
that cherished tone now detached
as if voice itself could be flung into space
without body
              At my kitchen table
The Toronto Star lies beside tall salt cellars
and where Bess Truman stares
with her closed gaze
                   Nadezhda Mandelstam's
Hope Against Hope, I notice, wears its purple
cover like a funeral robe.

Tonight in our cities no doubt some
one will cry out
            my daughter
sees in her dark room nameless horrors
and like photographs
               silent and distant
the dead will fall
             in the sum of
all days, nights, deaths, stars,
I hear this poem like a disembodied voice
less powerful than even a composition
made out of lead type and black ink

Envoi

my country is not a country
$\qquad\qquad$ but winter
rivers of ice
from St. Hubert terrible knives
run through the whiteness of my veins

politics pierce my heart
on a floor littered with history
I shiver while wardens shovel in
lunatic sentences, rag upon rag

it must be cold in prison, in québec

and your heart hurt singer
what do you see through its pane

icy slaves circle the river
montréal tense against the steel of its manacles
your words drifting like frozen wounds
$\qquad\qquad\qquad$ blessing
a sick bride
a murderous bridegroom
$\qquad\qquad\qquad$ that wedding
whose children will be colder killers
than the words of this or any other song

from *Out of Place*

the return:

in the estevan poem, for example,
how everyone can be seen eating
or is it reading
                    but not everyone
there is myself in the souris valley
forty years later
                    Ann
looking at wild flowers
cactus   their thick colours

I remember how I dreamt
her
        pale as a flower
        in the white sun
and in the dream
she is taking pictures

she photographs me
walking away
along a curving path
the flowers coloured
                    and
my father appears
my mother appears
saying no words
troubled
            and all
the ghostly jews
of estevan

praying
in the synagogue
of the valley
in the covenant
of coal mines
in these pictures
of estevan

signs:

and omens   windows
facing inward
            "an ideal
inserted into the plane
we call reality"   words
warning this is the place
you reach
        to name
remember and recite

the Hebrew alphabet
Invictus the first three
lines of Genesis
the unremembered man who stole
children from an empty town and
Latin   heroes in the hills and
glyphs uncles cousins step-
grandfather's sons and sisters

whatever has been hidden here
remains of speech
                the town lives
in its syntax we are ghosts

look   on the road beyond
mesas and moonscape
hoodoos   signs cut in rock
graffiti   gods
an indescribable border

doors of perception:

roads lead here   there
on the prairie Ann holds the Pinto
along great swoops of highway down
from Lloydminster past Batoche
rebellion Rudy's book researched
prophetic voices as a guide

in Huxley's version time curves
upon itself
                cities of the mescal dream
turned biblical   jeweled places
palaces of John in Revelation
Blake's engraving the drunkenness
of Smart's madness   prophecy

our history is in motion   curved
like straight correction lines
earth-measured on a western grid
place known through time   time
measuring place
                        Thompson walked
through unafraid for knowing
measurement and lore
                        ignorant
of clocks and vision we accelerate
a sweep through dying towns and farms

now is the badlands   measure
our choices random we believe
whatever we can find or where the map
of our own voices leads us listening to

the road to the cancer clinic
past the sundial's didacticism
toward the language of shadows
bedlam the alcoholic's nightmare
uses of wheat and rye and mould

strict farms die
beside the rails the roads
the sons construct
the rules of mind

the jewish exodus from shtetl to the plains
leads to this egypt abraham learned
dream-sickness and the way to heal
a place of bread and chemistry

madness is neither east nor north
Riel was hung in streets
I walked on every day to school

Note: Abraham Hoffer, son of Israel, is mentioned in a footnote to Huxley's *Doors of Perception and Heaven and Hell*. A psychiatrist, Abraham Hoffer has done pioneer work in the uses of lysergic acid as a means of exploring the nature and causes of schizophrenia and alcoholism. His father was a wheat farmer.

near Hirsch a Jewish cemetery:

ann is taking pictures again
while I stand in the uncut grass
counting the graves: there are forty
I think
          the Hebrew puzzles me
the wind moving the grass
over the still houses of the dead

from the road a muffled occasional
roar   cars passing   no one there
casts a glance at the stone trees
the unliving forest of Hebrew graves

in the picture I stand arms outstretched
as if waiting for someone
                         I am
in front of the gates you can see
the wind here   the grass
always bending the stone unmoved

STRIKE   sept 1931:

the coal miners stand in groups their faces like
Al Jolson's in Sonny Boy/they raise fists toward the
Chief of Police/he is wearing a blue uniform with
brass buttons on the jacket the red town hall at
his back and behind it the black water tower/the
siren at the top of the tower is blowing although it
isn't noon

the coal miners stand in groups their faces like
Al Jolson's in Sonny Boy/a woman in a long dress
raises both arms/she is shouting beside a touring
sedan/the Mounted Police come round the corner
on foot/they are dressed in brown jackets with Sam
Browne belts and brown trousers with a long yellow
stripe down the leg/they carry their pistols at
eye level

the coal miners run this way and that/one is falling
there is smoke around the guns of the Mounted Police/
windows are breaking/stones fly through the windows/
a coal miner with a face like Al Jolson's in Sonny
Boy is shouting

estevan, 1934:

remembering the family we
called breeds   the Roques
their house smelling of urine
my mother's prayers before
the dried fish she cursed
them for their dirtiness their
women I remember too
                                how
seldom they spoke and
they touched one another

even when the sun killed
cattle and rabbis
                        even
in poisoned slow air
like hunters
                like lizards
they touched   stone
they touched
                earth

petroglyphs at st victor:

1

watching the sun
watching the sun's wheel
great slow metaphors
wheel toward me out of the sun

they take my eyes from my head
they place my eyes on rocks
they take my crying tongue
they wheel back toward the sun
their black hands carrying my name

now my drawings of god
look no better than my child's
drawing of me
                I remember
the sun   his arms flailing
wheat and skin   his mouth
warning of hollows and gulleys
one eye grinning   news
about crossings
              I try feet now
get the toes wrong
forget the signals once again

whether the snake's head
points inside or outside the sun
for circling the snake ridge

I've always been wrong
about metaphors
about the five figures
of discourse
                 the seventy
names of rhetoric and tree
alphabets
                 when they gave me
my name I knew the only one
to follow me would mistake
my image/sign
                 all the others
praising the gods

2

the crooked gods:

>   do they mean anything?
>   I ask Ann
>   parkland
>   rolling below sandstone
>
>   silent
>   she turns
>   the camera
>   here
>   there
>   I kneel
>   before the crooked gods
>
>   last light wheeling
>   over the land
>   their handprints
>   their great feet
>   their stone faces
>   move
>   turning
>   we leave
>   take with us
>   photographs
>   silent
>   as
>   their open mouths

3

below the petroglyphs
separate as Quebec
St Victor maintains
direction
          in badlands
four horses on a hill
become a black turmoil
scattered gravel on a road
somersaulting birds
another god
hangs on his cross
near Gravelbourg

we drive through names:
Coronach Canopus Constance
Big Beaver Hart Ceylon Glasnevin
Ogema Horizon Assiniboia
La Fleche McCord Mankota
Stonehenge Montagu
Readlyn Willow Bunch
Dahindel Wheatstone Crystal Hill
Galilee Truax Amulet
Pangman Khedive
                    until

Point Alison
where the super-continental stands
our children crying out
barely glimpse redness a form
the end of names and aesthetics

later
amid wreckage of slippers
licorice I remember the cut
god's mouths at Wood Mountain
rhetoric of stone its bluntness

Ann
talking
about children
tomorrow
our return
home
train time

the doppelganger:

ways to prevent me:

refusing to be interrupted especially by children
single-mindedness to the point of brutality
in all matters of politics religion metaphysics &
the character and lives of your closest friends
praising the worst lines of your fellow writers
jogging followed by volley ball and cold showers
concentrated masturbation before and after sex
sleeping with a towel knotted in your back
inspired teaching ferocious tactics in rumoli
combinations of alcohol librium and   bad novels

seeing I'm here you know all methods fail
you don't even know how long it has been
what I might have said to children or others
now it's forever too late
no one could possibly know
you've been gone for days
when I make love to your wife
she will moan and praise you
asking you never to leave

where shall I say you have gone?

Pictures in an Institution

1

Notice: all mirrors will be covered
the mailman is forbidden to speak
professors are confined to their offices
faculties no longer exist.

2

I speak of what I know,
how uncle Asher, spittle on his lips,
first typed with harvest hands the fox
across a fence and showing all good men
come to their country's aid rushed off to Israel
there to brutalize his wife and son

how step-grandfather Barak wiped
sour curds out of his curly beard
before he roared the Sabbath in my ears
what Sara, long his widow, dreamed
the night she cried: God, let him die at last,
thinking perhaps of Josef who had lost
jewels in Russia where the Cossack rode
but coughed his stomach out in Winnipeg

Your boredom does not matter. I take,
brutal to my thoughts, these lives, defy
your taste in metaphor; the wind-break
on the farm that Barak plowed to dust
makes images would ruin public poetry.

The rites of love I knew:
how father cheated brother, uncle, son,
and bankrupt-grocer, that we might eat
wrote doggerel verse, later took his wife,
my mother, in the English way beside my bed.
Why would he put his Jewishness aside?
Because there was no bread?

                              Or out of spite
that doctors sliced his double rupture,
fingered spleen, and healed his bowel's ache?

Lovers lie down in glades, are glad.
These, now in graves, their headstones sunk,
knew nothing of such marvels, only God, his ways,
owning no texts of Greek or anthropology.

                    3

Notice: the library is closed to all who read
           any student carrying a gun
           registers first, exempt from fines,
           is given thirteen books per month,
           one course in science, one in math,
           two options
                        campus police
           will see to co-ed's underwear

4

These names I rehearse:
                    Eva, Isaac,
Charley, Yetta, Max
                    now dead
or dying or beyond my lies

till I reeling with messages
and sick to hold again their bitter lives
put them, with shame, into my poetry.

5

Notice: there will be no further communication
           lectures are cancelled
           all students are expelled
           the reading of poetry is declared a public crime

On the Murder of Salvador Allende

1

hopeless + remote
you peer from a balcony
your voice light as a girl's voice
                 your face
now that I look at it closely
not a pale petal   a photograph

under the flower of your face
it says here   in this unreliable
newspaper   you cried out
at last to your people

did you allow yourself
an impossible vision
                all your countrymen
marching in rows towards guns and armour
embracing the soldiers   drowning
the colonels   with kisses and flowers

or did you
fated and tough old marxist
turn back to your desk
look again at rows of figures
                deficits   demands
the hemorrhage of capital and reserves
the streets bloody   your people defeated

2

this photograph shows a gun
silently exploding
                    there are
above the city mountains
something that looks like a man
leans out of a palace window

3

I have been taught an intricate
love of efficient death

I respond with appropriate gestures
as in this elegy
                    funeral rites
for a doctor distant and unknown
my poetry itself serving the state
with its celebration of your murder

4

twice only have I met your compatriots   doctor
once in Regina a distant cousin who taught me
Neruda
            and in Toledo by the banks of the Tagus
the night sky brilliant with flowers of light
a dark boy his hands supple   singing

I know nothing of your history your people
your cause
            only a bad story about words
spoken at the coffin of your father

only this image of palaces and knives
the silent explosion of guns

it changes nothing: it goes on:
today in Omonia Square guns in the mouth of speech
yesterday in Mozambique
                        the same taste
of death and torture
                        admirals calculating
losses and reserves

                5

it may be   in the mines of your country
a dark face looks up briefly

in the hills remote and aloof or dully
an Indian stares at the sky

        do they remember names
        do they remember the morning of the death squad
        what stood there on the palace steps

        the morning of the death squad
        the morning of Lorca's death
        how out of bullets in his mouth poems flowered?

The Madwomen of the Plaza de Mayo

They wear white scarves and shawls.
They carry pictures on strings about their necks.
I have seen their faces elsewhere:
in Ereceira, fishermen's wives
walking in dark processions
to the sea, its roaring,
women of Ireland
wearing their dark scarves
hearing the echo of guns, bombs

Identities
the *desaparecidos*
lost ones
the disappeared

in the Plaza the Presidential Palace
reveals soldiers like fences with steel spikes
the rhythm of lost bodies
the rhythm of loss

A soldier is a man who is not a man.
A fence, a spike
A nail in somebody's eye.
Lost man.

Why are the women weeping?
For whom do they cry
under the orange moon
under the lemon moon of Buenos Aires?

"If only for humanitarian reasons
tell the families of the living
where are they
tell the families of the dead
what they need
what they deserve to know."

No one speaks.
The junta says nothing.
The *desaparecidos* remain silent.
The moon has no language.

In My 57th Year

This is the year my mother lay dying
knocked down by tiny strokes she claimed
never once hit her though when she lay
crib-like where they laid her there she wept
for shame to be confined so near her death.
This is the year the cancer inside my father's
groin began its growth to knock him down
strong as he was beside his stricken wife.
This is the year I grew, ignorant of politics,
specious with law, careless of poetry.
There were no graves. The prairie rolled on
as if it were the sea. Today my children make
their way alone across those waves.
Do lines between us end as sharply
as lines our artists draw upon the plains?
I cry out. They keep their eye upon
their politics, their myths,
careful of lives as I was careless.

What shall I say? It is too late to tell again
tales we never knew. The legends of ourselves
spill into silence. All we never said, father
to daughter, son to unmanned man, we cannot say
to count the years.
         I no longer know time or age
thinking of parents, their time, their grave of names.
Telling the time fiction consumes me.

Zenith: Saving to Disk

This poem will be saved
a saved poem can not be made up out
of lines that will not remain
invisible or words that wont
dissolve—the illusion will
at last become the reality

or will it become real because
it has become print and not
these ghostly flickering
figures on a screen

figures on a screen
illusions dreams
of words dreamt by me:

the absence of my self
the absent self who writes
the ghostly writing self

the ghost writer

dreaming his own holocaust
himself the victim and his own
executioner

[Computer poem on Zenith 148, Draft Three]

Afterword

I sat in on Eli Mandel's graduate class in Canadian poetry at York University in 1982–83. At one point, Eli mischievously interrupted the discussion to ask, "What do you remember when you're remembering?"

Somebody offered, tentatively, "The past."

"Right," Eli nodded. "So what is it you imagine when you're imagining?" Somebody came up with "The future."

"That's very Jungian, very Christian," Eli said. (Not to mention very Northrop Frye—whose mythopoetics was once regarded as a decisive influence on Mandel's work). "You know, for me it's the other way around. I dream the past and remember the future—that's Freudian."

Remembering the future is about re-entering, and rereading, old landscapes, places that have been visited or dwelled in before but abandoned—one remembers "forward" into new terrain that looks oddly familiar. The latest encounter is driven by a sense of unfinished business. It calls up memory but fragmented memory, foreshadowings of the past. This is a dream-like feeling of the uncanny: the *unheimlich*. It is a landscape of partial glimpses, traces, symptom formations. (Macbeth, who stands over *Black and Secret Man*, does not know Birnam Wood has always already come to Dunsinane. He forgets he has been through it before—lived, killed, died. Only now, *after* the end, can the play begin.) Similarly, Mandel's early books are new trespasses into the labyrinth of myth, re-encounters with literary forebears. He dedicated *Dreaming Backwards*, his selected poems, to his mother and "all my fathers." "Fathers" are the poets of the English tradition.[1] This mythology floats above, and masks, an existential post-Holocaust void; in "Auschwitz and Poetry," Mandel describes his return to Estevan in August 1946 after his army service in World War II:

> Among other things, I was expected to visit an uncle and aunt in Estevan, the town where I had been born and brought up, to tell them of my last moments with their son in London, England, three weeks before his death in Europe, in Normandy. I was the last of the family to see him alive. On the way to Estevan, I stopped at his sister's house in Weyburn. There, on an oppressively hot summer day, alone in the house, moody, depressed, I picked up a book, idly glancing at its introduction. It was Thomas Mann's "Introduction" to *The Short Novels of Dostoevsky*. The words leaped at me

from the page. Mann is defending Nietzsche's position in *The Birth of Tragedy*. ("Auschwitz" 4)

He is struck by Mann's paradox that "life has never been able to do without the morbid. . . . Life is not prudish and it is probably safe to say that life prefers creative genius-bestowing disease a thousand times over to prosaic health . . . certain attainments of the soul are impossible without disease, without insanity, without spiritual crime" (qtd. in Mandel, "Auschwitz" 5). "The reversal—sanity-health/insanity-poetry, illness-poetry/health-prose—" was, Mandel tells us, "stunning" (5). "That night, at Weyburn, I wrote what I knew to be my first poem, 'Estevan Saskatchewan.' It was ten years before I fully understood the implications of that moment, and almost another ten years before I could possibly begin to undertake the task of attempting an account of where I believed the real obscenity stood" (5).

In "Estevan Saskatchewan," home space is distorted by darkness, impotence.

A small town bears the mark of Cain,
Or the oldest brother with the dead king's wife
In a foul relation as viewed by sons,
Lies on the land, squat, producing
Love's queer offspring only,
Which issue drives the young
To feign a summer madness, consort with skulls,
While the farmer's chorus, a Greek harbinger,
Forecasts by frost or rings around the moon
How ill and black the seeds will grow.

Mandel's memories of Europe in ruins, and the loss of his cousin Jake in August 1944, forge a homecoming that is also not a homecoming: significantly, the poem is written during a "stopover." He carries the memory/trace of having already left. The "gaps" in the field are signs of his absence, delayed return—hence the prophecies ("forecasts") of madness, death. Meanwhile, we get images of incest, "lies," and botched birth. And there are the tricks and feints of language—puns, the multiplied meanings of words. History falls apart, and the poem becomes, self-consciously, also about its own impossibility. Don't forget, Mandel's career begins far away from home, in fact in Toronto. "Estevan Saskatchewan" appeared in *Trio* (1954), his first book. (It was at Contact Press, at Louis Dudek's command, that "E.W. Mandel" became "Eli Mandel." "It was Louis Dudek who named me," Eli recalled.) Mandel writes himself "back" home, or in the direction of home, through ensuing books. All this culminates in his belated mid-1970s re-return, with

Ann, to the South Saskatchewan of his childhood, documented in *Out of Place* (1977).

Fuseli Poems (1960) and *Black and Secret Man* (1964) are likewise second sojourns. Their worlds are Gothic, and they call up ghosts of Henry Fuseli, Macbeth, and Christopher Smart's feminine "other," Mary Midnight. Always literature is implicated in the catastrophe of history: genocide. This pathology is on display in the Governor General's Award–winning *An Idiot Joy* (1967). Later books continue the pattern of repetition-encountering-displacement. Doubleness is duplicity: the image in the mirror as identity and reversal. But later books extend Mandel's political vision. Incrementally we move from private pasts to public pasts. The scene of writing becomes global, and the doubles we meet are the "others" of history. *Stony Plain* (1973) is McLuhanesque: it addresses language as medium, as technology. (In fact, its working title was "War Measures." One inspiration was Mandel's meeting with Pierre Trudeau, F.R. Scott, and others at Ramsay Cook's home in Toronto in November 1970. This was, of course, during the wind-down to the Quebec crisis.)[2] *Out of Place* is about space—memory as space/place, as landscape. *Life Sentence* (1981) returns to scenes of political oppression, revolution, and war. It re-dramatizes the complicity of speech/writing in violence. Repetition, for Mandel, is always accompanied by difference—and this may be poetry's saving grace. It is not just what to say but when to say it: timing is all. As Eli once commented, "I won't write a book just to repeat myself; I won't write till I have something new to say."

Mandel's poetry is consistently psychologically penetrating, and the mythologies and literary resonances of his earliest work are not neutral (or "overdetermined") signifiers. They are attempts to get at the deeper motives of the anti-social mindset, and the desire to pervert or destroy is not far removed from the need to write: insanity thinks like poetry. Indeed, criminal acts have a certain aesthetic appeal; they can be seen as masterpieces (the Nazi high command had a taste for art). Incidentally, Mandel encountered Sigmund Freud via Lionel Trilling's essay "Freud and Literature," in *The Liberal Imagination* (1950), and his use of myth is Freudian in the sense of its being attached to sickness. Freud, don't forget, named complexes after myths (Oedipus, Narcissus), foregrounding the dangers of living in fiction. (When I first said I was interested in doing a full-length study of his work, Eli reacted: "Well, okay, but you're going to have to read all of Freud!")

So one of the major icons of Mandel's poetics—the ever-returning Double—has a psychological/psychoanalytical resonance: the Double is the carrier of order and chaos, perversion and genius, silence and speech. Meeting one's Double heralds the onset of creative power or death, and the outcome of the meeting is chancy. Mandel's Double prefigures the "heroic" outlaw figures that turn up as Michael Ondaatje's Billy the Kid, Paulette Jiles's Jesse James, Dennis Cooley's Bloody Jack, and Rienzi Crusz's Sardiel. The Double also represents the collision of sophistication and vulgarity, the academic and the primitive. Mandel documents this in the figure of the "savage critic." In his critical study *Criticism: The Silent-Speaking Words* (1966), the refinements of Anglo-modernism encounter the dislocations of alternate canons and revolutionary (American) pop culture. This is part of his lifelong interest in the eroticism of cultural "primitives" like Irving Layton and Leonard Cohen.

In fact, his attraction to the academic–popular binary probably goes back to the split he inherited from Canada's twin modernisms, the high-modernist metaphysical sophistications of the Montreal/McGill movement and John Sutherland's streetwise—realist/leftist—"Brooklyn-Bum" poetics (59). At the same time, Mandel's savage critic is situated in the "dialogue" between the courtly and murderous (and failed) artist Salieri and the brilliant but uncouth Mozart in Peter Shaffer's *Amadeus*, a version of the Sartre–Genet doublet Mandel evokes in "The Poet as Liar":

> Is it so difficult to imagine the vertigo Sartre must have felt on seeing in the language of the criminal, himself? And in the literature of fantasy the language he as philosopher had laboured so hard to forge? A world in which one thing could become another, not in fact, but in dream (or myth, the self-creating fabulous world opened up in language). How baffling that these fabulous dislocations should be given to an obsequious, cringing, vulgar little man, the very picture of a humiliation so profound that we can do nothing but suspect it. (18)

A signature poem in *An Idiot Joy*, published a year after *Criticism: The Silent-Speaking Words*, is "Houdini," where we encounter the savage critic, who dwells in the cracks between pieces of a broken past, between tradition and its "others," and between outside and inside, as master escape artist. The Houdini of the poem is eventually the voice of the poet, which is why the various traps, gadgets, and toys—all domestic artifacts—Houdini plays with are, finally, words. Poetry is a game, where the object is to escape from language itself; but, ironically, this is only in order to return to the very verbal constructs, chains ("metaphors") he left behind:

> I suspect he knew that trunks are metaphors,
> could distinguish between the finest rhythms
> unrolled on rope or singing in a chain
> and knew the metrics of the deepest pools

The freedom–bondage overlap implies an obsessive-compulsive relationship with words, not only words in their "raw" (given? primordial? innocent?) form but in their state of having been uttered before. Words are not naive: they harbour the voices of other poets, and so come to him as, in the classic sense, topoi. They are localities, "commonplaces," already saturated with meaning. Thus the new poem can appear as endless citation, or recitation, or as taxonomy. The spaces between words also show as stitches in the fabric. So silence itself becomes a feature of the text, to be spoken, read. We always know, self-consciously, guiltily, it *is* a poem—that is, "merely" a poem. This suggests a major tension in Mandel's writing. Harold Bloom (one of Mandel's favourite critics) calls this "the anxiety of influence." From this angle, every poem becomes the site of an Oedipal struggle between a strong "precursor" poet and a weak belated poet ("ephebe"). This struggle can be seen in repetitions (Milton's "Sin"), which for Mandel are also points of contradiction or resistance (Milton's "Death").

The contest between these forces becomes the foundational interpretive as well as creative economy in Mandel's work. This internal power struggle invites us, again, to read Mandel as a political writer. His connection/disconnect is the at times fraught, at times symbiotic relation of critic to poet. This is also the relation of meaning to creation, poetry to prose. Mandel always wanted his poetry to be understood in light of his prose, and vice versa. His writing has at different times, in different ways, been a pursuit of origin. Possibly this has been, in the end, only a *dream* of origin. The discovery he makes in his last poetry book, *Life Sentence*, is through a combination of poems and prose travel journals. The discovery is that origin is not in time but place, in fact place as "other." "The world," he tells us, "begins to begin *elsewhere*" ("May 15" 363).

However, Mandel's visits to such places change his role: he is at last, more than in earlier books, the "receiver" and transcriber of information, given to him by the *else*-world he moves through, as he moves through it. The precision, "accuracy," of his accounts of what he sees is therefore an act of restoration. Finally, like Orestes, he sees order put back—ironically, without anything having changed. In this sense, the world is the author of itself, but it is a world that offers itself to him, without secrets and without depth: what remains is surface, rhetoric.

—*Andrew Stubbs*

Notes

1 Notice the replication of the father icon in the expression "all my fathers." For Eli, as for Freud, whom Eli thought of as a "great mythic thinker," repetition is tied to dismemberment—in effect castration. "Houdini," Eli told me, is "an Oedipal poem." Eli once travelled to the Ukraine,

to the area around Kiev, in search of the village his father had grown up in and from which his father had emigrated to Canada. He gave the name of the village to his tour guide, who laughed: there were, apparently, hundreds of villages in the area around Kiev with that name. Again the image is of duplication, a kind of geographical dismantling of his genealogy. In his later poetry, his mother plays a much larger role in his birthing/naming as a poet. The poem "birthmark" (*Out of Place*) plays on the name of the river running through Estevan: souris/mouse:

> seeing a mouse
> my mother struck her temple
>
> he'll be marked at birth
> she said
> > the women cried
>
> I carry the souris
> on my brow
> > the river
> in my head
> > the valley
> of my dreams
> still echoes
> with her cry

2 See English 100–2.

Works Cited

English, John. *Just Watch Me: The Life of Pierre Elliott Trudeau, 1968–2000.* Toronto: Knopf, 2009. Print.

Mandel, Eli. "Auschwitz and Poetry." *The Family Romance.* Winnipeg: Turnstone, 1986. 3–10. Print.

———. "Birthmark." *Other Harmony* 244.

———. *Criticism: The Silent-Speaking Words.* Toronto: CBC, 1966. Print.

———. *Dreaming Backwards.* Don Mills, ON: General, 1981. Print.

———. "May 15. Victoria." *Other Harmony* 363–64.

———. *The Other Harmony: The Collected Poetry of Eli Mandel.* Ed. Andrew Stubbs and Judy Chapman. Vol. 1. Regina: Canadian Plains Research Center, 2000. Print.

———. "The Poet as Liar." *Another Time.* Erin, ON: Press Porcépic, 1977. 15–24. Print.

Sutherland, John. "Introduction to *Other Canadians.*" *The Making of Modern Poetry in Canada.* Ed. Louis Dudek and Michael Gnarowski. Toronto: Ryerson, 1967. 47–61. Print.

Acknowledgements

The editors and the publisher gratefully acknowledge Ann Mandel for her permission to reprint the poems listed below. Peter Webb also wishes to thank Dean Irvine, Director of Editing Modernism in Canada (EMiC), and Melanie Dennis Unrau, research assistant at The University of Winnipeg, for their help in bringing this volume to fruition.

From *Trio* (Toronto: Contact Press, 1954)
    Minotaur Poems
    Estevan Saskatchewan

From *Fuseli Poems* (Toronto: Contact Press, 1960)
    The Fire Place
    In the Caves of My City
    City Park Merry-Go-Round
    Doll on the Mantelpiece
    Epilogue

From *Black and Secret Man* (Toronto: Ryerson, 1964)
    Mary Midnight's Prologue (also in *Mary Midnight*)
    Charles Isaac Mandel
    David
    Hippolytus

From *An Idiot* Joy (Edmonton: M.G. Hurtig, 1967)
    The Meaning of the I CHING
    Girl on a High Wire
    Houdini
    The Madness of Our Polity
    The Speaking Earth
    From the North Saskatchewan

From *Stony Plain* (Erin, ON: Porcépic, 1973)
    Two Dream Songs for John Berryman
    On the 25th Anniversary of the Liberation of Auschwitz
    Room XV

On the Renewal of Bombing in VietNam December, 1972
Envoi

From *Out of Place* (Erin, ON: Porcépic, 1977)
    the return
    signs [untitled in first edition]
    doors of perception
    near Hirsch a Jewish cemetery
    STRIKE sept 1931
    estevan, 1934 (also in *Stony Plain*)
    petroglyphs at st victor
    the doppelganger
    Pictures in an Institution (also in *An Idiot Joy*)

From *Life Sentence: Poems and Journals, 1976-1980* (Victoria: Porcépic, 1981)
    On the Murder of Salvador Allende
    The Madwomen of the Plaza de Mayo
    In My 57th Year

From *The Other Harmony: The Collected Poetry of Eli Mandel*. Volume 2
(Regina: Canadian Plains Research Center, 2000)
    Zenith: Saving to Disk

lps Books in the Laurier Poetry Series

Published by Wilfrid Laurier University Press

Eli Mandel   *From Room to Room: The Poetry of Eli Mandel*, edited by Peter Webb, with an afterword by Andrew Stubbs • 2011 • xviii + 66 pp. • ISBN 978-1-55458-255-6

Steve McCaffery *Verse and Worse: Selected and New Poems of Steve McCaffery 1989–2009*, edited by Darren Wershler, with an afterword by Steve McCaffery • 2010 • xiv + 76 pp. • ISBN 978-1-55458-188-7

Don McKay   *Field Marks: The Poetry of Don McKay*, edited by Méira Cook, with an afterword by Don McKay • 2006 • xxvi + 60 pp. • ISBN-10: 0-88920-494-2; ISBN-13: 978-0-88920-494-2

Al Purdy   *The More Easily Kept Illusions: The Poetry of Al Purdy*, edited by Robert Budde, with an afterword by Russell Brown • 2006 • xvi + 80 pp. • ISBN-10: 0-88920-490-X; ISBN-13: 978-0-88920-490-4

Fred Wah   *The False Laws of Narrative: The Poetry of Fred Wah*, edited by Louis Cabri, with an afterword by Fred Wah • 2009 • xxiv + 78 pp. • ISBN 978-1-555458-046-0